Oct. 04

On

World Book, Inc.
180 North LaSalle Street
Suite 900
Chicago, Illinois 60601
USA

For information about other World Book publications, visit our website at **http://www.worldbook.com** or call **1-800-WORLDBK (967-5325)**.

For information about sales to schools and libraries, call **1-800-975-3250 (United States)**; **1-800-837-5365 (Canada)**.

2008 revised printing

**Library of Congress Cataloging-in-Publication Data**

On the move.
    p. cm. -- (World Book's learning ladders)
    Summary: "Introduction to modes of transportation using simple text, question and answer format, illustrations, and photos. Features include puzzles and games, fun facts, a resource list, and an index"--Provided by publisher.
    Includes bibliographical references and index.
    ISBN 978-0-7166-7728-4
    1. Transportation--Miscellanea--Juvenile literature.    I. World Book, Inc.
    TA1149.O58 2007
    629.04--dc22
                        2007018910

World Book's Learning Ladders
Set ISBN: 978-0-7166-7725-3 (print)

E-book editions:
ISBN 978-0-7166-7756-7 (Learning Hub)
ISBN 978-0-7166-7757-4 (Spindle)
ISBN 978-0-7166-7758-1 (EPUB3)
ISBN 978-0-7166-7759-8 (PDF)

Printed in China by Shenzhen Wing King Tong Paper Products Co, Ltd., Shenzhen, Guangdong
9th printing June 2016

Editor in Chief: Paul A. Kobasa

Supplementary Publications
    Associate Director: Scott Thomas
    Managing Editor: Barbara A. Mayes

Senior Editor: Shawn Brennan

Editor: Dawn Krajcik

Researcher: Cheryl Graham

Manager, Contracts & Compliance
    (Rights & Permissions): Loranne K. Shields

Graphics and Design
    Associate Director: Sandra M. Dyrlund
    Associate Manager, Design: Brenda B. Tropinski
    Associate Manager, Photography: Tom Evans

Production
    Director, Manufacturing and Pre-Press: Carma Fazio
    Manager, Manufacturing: Steven Hueppchen
    Production Technology Manager: Anne Fritzinger
    Proofreader: Emilie Schrage

This edition is an adaptation of the Ladders series published originally by T&N Children's Publishing, Inc., of Minnetonka, Minnesota.

**Photographic credits:** Cover: © Michael DeYoung, Corbis; p4: Allsport UK Ltd; p5: Telegraph Colour Library; p7: Quadrant Picture Library; p9 top: Robert Harding Picture Library; bottom: © Jeremy Hoare, Alamy Images; p10: James Davis Travel Photography; p12: AP/Wide World; p13: Pictor International; p17: Britstock-IFA; p18: Zefa; p19: Tony Stone Images; p21: Tony Stone Images; p22: Tony Stone Images; p23: © Stephen Strathdee, Shutterstock.

**Illustrators:** Gaëtan Evrard, Jon Stuart

# What's inside?

This book tells you about lots of exciting ways to travel. You can find out how cars and trains speed over land, how boats float across water, how airplanes soar through the sky, and more!

 4 Bicycle

 6 Car

 8 Bus

 10 Truck

 12 Train

 14 Moving along

 16 Small boat

 18 Ship

 20 Helicopter

 22 Airplane

 24 Sea and sky

 26 Did you know?

 28 Puzzles

 30 True or false

 31 Find out more

 32 Answers and Index

# Bicycle

Bicycles are lots of fun. You can cycle to the park with your friends or to the store. It is easy to learn how to ride a bicycle. You may wobble at first, but soon you will be pedaling like a pro!

A lightweight racing bicycle speeds along a track. The rider dips his body and head, letting the air rush past.

Two **wheels** spin around and move the bicycle forward.

Always wear a hard **helmet** to protect your head.

To ride a bicycle, you sit on the seat and push the **pedals** with your feet.

A **mudguard** helps keep you dry when you splash through a puddle.

Holding the **handlebars** keeps you steady and lets you steer.

You can ring your **bell** to warn people that you are coming.

A rickshaw has three wheels and a comfortable back seat. You sit inside and a driver cycles you across town.

When you squeeze the brake on the handlebar, a **brake pad** rubs against the wheel to slow you down.

## It's a fact!

A unicycle has one wheel and no handlebars. It takes time and a lot of balance to learn how to ride one!

 # Car

All over the world, people travel by car. A car can hold a whole family, and it can go wherever there are roads. Cars are quick, too, but watch out—there may be a traffic jam ahead!

Turning the **steering wheel** makes the car turn left or right.

An **engine** uses fuel to make the car move.

At night, the car's bright **headlights** light up the road.

Thick **tires** grip the road, even in wet weather.

You can pile extra luggage onto the **roof rack**.

A race car zooms around a track as fast as it can. Before the race, a team of helpers checks that the car works properly.

Everybody helps load luggage into the **trunk** for the journey.

Wearing a **seat belt** helps keep you safe.

 # Bus

Buses pick people up and drop them off at bus stops all over town. There is room for lots of people inside. As you ride the bus, you can look out the windows and watch for your stop.

You wait for a bus at a **bus stop**.

You read the **schedule** to find out when your bus will arrive.

Inside, the **passengers** sit on seats or stand.

The **doors** open to let everybody climb on board.

You need to pay **money** for your ride.

A **sign** tells you where the bus is going.

TOWN SQUARE

The **driver** can see the road clearly through the big front windows.

A minibus is full inside, so people tie their packages to the roof!

A double-decker bus chugs through the city. You can sit down below or climb upstairs to the seats on top.

# Truck

Trucks come in different shapes and sizes. They rumble down roads, moving all kinds of heavy loads from place to place. Trucks can deliver ice-cold drinks and fresh bread to a shop or take your furniture to a new home.

This long truck carries oil in two huge, shiny containers. The driver travels for days to deliver the load.

There is plenty of space inside the **trailer** to pile up your belongings.

Packing things in strong **boxes** keeps them safe.

Movers walk down a **ramp** to reach the ground.

The front part of the truck is called the **cab**. This is where the driver and a helper sit.

## It's a fact!

The world's highest truck has wheels taller than two adults. You reach the cab by climbing up a ladder!

A large **mirror** makes it easy for the driver to see the road behind him.

Movers climb up a **step** to get into the cab.

A sofa is a heavy **load**. It is hard work carrying it to the house!

# Train

All day long, trains hurry from town to town. They stop at stations along the way to let people step on and off. A train moves quickly, racing past fields, over bridges, and through deep, dark tunnels.

This is the maglev, the world's fastest train. It rushes people around at speeds of up to six times that of a car on a highway.

Passengers sit in **coaches** that are hooked together in a long line.

Zooming through a **tunnel** in a mountain is faster than trudging up and over a mountain.

A train rolls along two shiny rails called **railroad tracks**.

The engineer moves **levers** to make the train speed up or slow down.

Underground trains, sometimes called subways, shoot through tunnels far beneath a big city.

A powerful **locomotive** pulls or pushes the train forward.

Bright **lights** help the driver see ahead and let people know the train is coming.

**Wheels** with special edges keep the train on the track.

# Moving along

Today the town is packed with lots of people going to different places. They are in cars, trucks, and buses, and on bikes!

How many people are riding bicycles?

14

Which car looks like it has engine trouble?

# Words you know

Here are words that you read earlier in this book. Say them out loud, then try to find the things in the picture.

**passengers  trailer  wheels
coaches      helmet  engine**

15

# Small boat

Floating on the water in a small boat is great fun. You can sit in a sailboat, like the one in the big picture, and let the wind blow you gently along. A sailboat often tips and rolls in the waves, so remember to hold on tight!

A **life jacket** helps keep you safe if you fall into the water.

The wind blows against a large **sail** and pushes the boat forward.

To move the sail, you pull on a thick **rope**.

You move the **rudder** to make the sailboat turn.

A tall, strong **mast** holds up the sail.

Paddling a kayak can be hard work! You push the long paddle through the water to move the boat along.

The **hold** is a good place to store a picnic basket!

The **hull** floats in the water. There is room for a few people to sit inside.

# It's a fact!

Speedboats have powerful engines and can go extremely fast. Sometimes, when they hit a wave, they jump right out of the water!

 # Ship

Ships are giant boats. Many ships cross the big oceans from one side of the world to the other. Ferries, like the one in the big picture, carry people on short journeys. One end opens up to let people drive on board.

## It's a fact!

Oil tankers are among the world's longest ships. You would need a bicycle to travel from one end to the other!

A cruise ship slowly glides through the warm, blue sea. It is taking hundreds of people on a faraway vacation.

People park their cars on the **car deck**.

People wait at the **dock** before driving onto the ferry.

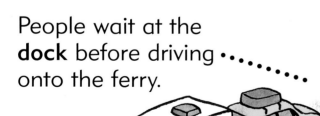

Smoke puffs out of the **smokestack**.

The **captain** is in charge of the ferry and steers it out of the dock.

On the **top deck**, you can sit on seats and chat.

From inside, you can look out of large **portholes**.

This cargo ship carries heavy boxes packed with goods. Huge cranes lift the boxes onto the ship.

# Helicopter

Have you ever seen a helicopter whirling in the sky? It can fly straight up and down and even hover (stay in one place in the air). Helicopters have many jobs. Some help people watch the traffic below, others take people sightseeing!

A **headset** lets the pilot talk to people on the ground.

A **pilot** sits at the front and flies the helicopter.

The pilot moves a **joy stick** to make the helicopter go up and down or stay still.

## It's a fact!

A helicopter can land in a small space. It can even squeeze onto the top of a high building in a busy city.

The helicopter lands gently on its two strong **skids**.

Flat **blades** whirl around and lift the helicopter into the air.

This helicopter carries people to work at sea and takes them home many months later. It lands on a special platform called a helipad.

A long **tail** with spinning blades at the end keeps the helicopter steady.

Passengers sit in the bubble-shaped **cabin** and look at the amazing view!

# Airplane

Airplanes take off and land at airports. They fly high above the clouds, carrying people to different cities and countries. In an airplane, you can fly across the world in a day!

These decorated airplanes take part in an air show. They fly side by side, twisting and turning in the sky.

A baggage truck carries piles of suitcases to the **hold**.

Huge **wings** help the airplane soar through the air.

An airplane speeds along the runway and **takes off**.

A pilot sits high up in the **cockpit** behind the controls.

Passengers climb up the steps and a **flight attendant** welcomes them on board.

An airplane has strong **wheels** to help it land smoothly on the runway.

23

# Sea and sky

The sea and sky are full of people moving about! Some are having fun and others are going on a journey.

## Words you know

Here are some words that you learned earlier. Say them out loud, then try to find the things in the picture.

| | | |
|---|---|---|
| rudder | wings | sail |
| portholes | car deck | cabin |

Where do cars and trucks wait before driving onto the ferry?

Where is the helicopter pilot?

# Did you know?

In some countries, more people ride bicycles than drive cars because it costs far less to ride a bike.

*Car* comes from a Latin word that means *four-wheeled cart*.

Americans drive over 2 ¾ trillion miles (4.4 trillion kilometers) a year.

The word *helicopter* comes from Greek words meaning *spiral* and *wing.* Nicknames for the helicopter include "chopper," "eggbeater," and "whirlybird."

The difference between a ship and a boat is mainly size. Large vessels that travel on the ocean are called *ships.* All other craft are called *boats.*

*Kayak* is an Inuit word. The Inuit, Aleuts, and Yuit of the Arctic regions made kayaks more than 6,000 years ago.

# True or false

Can you figure out which of these facts are true? You can turn to the page numbers listed to help you find the answers.

The world's highest truck has wheels taller than two adults.
**Go to page 11.**

3

A helicopter can land in a city on the top of a high building.
**Go to page 20.**

1

A unicycle is a bicycle with three wheels.
**Go to page 5.**

4

A speedboat whizzes along really fast underwater.
**Go to page 17.**

2

The world's longest car has a swimming pool on-board.
**Go to page 6.**

5

Answers on page 32.